T0129544

Sasha, Butch, Cuff and Seff

Sasha, Butch, Cuff and Seff

Friends' Journey in Saving Earth

Glengyl Onga Umali

Sustainable Community Development Advocate

iUniverse

SASHA, BUTCH, CUFF AND SEFF
FRIENDS' JOURNEY IN SAVING EARTH

iUniverse books may be ordered through booksellers or by contacting:

iUniverse
1663 Liberty Drive
Bloomington, IN 47403
www.iuniverse.com
1-800-Authors (1-800-288-4677)

Because of the dynamic nature of the Internet, any web addresses or
links contained in this book may have changed since publication and may
no longer be valid. The views expressed in this work are solely those of
the author and do not necessarily reflect the views of the publisher,
and the publisher hereby disclaims any responsibility for them.

Any people depicted in stock imagery provided by Getty Images are
models, and such images are being used for illustrative purposes only.
Certain stock imagery © Getty Images.

ISBN: 978-1-5320-9133-9 (sc)
ISBN: 978-1-5320-9134-6 (e)

Print information available on the last page.

iUniverse rev. date: 12/28/2019

An Activity Book for Children

Short Story | Sketching | Coloring Book | Team Building Activity Guide

Contents

Contents

Introduction

This book is for all the Kids out there who dreamed of having a sustainable environment, free from pollution and how to be a responsible citizen of the Earth!

Featuring a Short Story of friends Sasha, Butch, Cuff and Seff and their journey of becoming an Earth Warrior. A multi-activity book from coloring, sketching, trivia, puzzles and quizzes, and lastly the ABC of Single-used Plastics.

This will educate kids on the impacts of using single use plastics + Bonus Activity Guide for Teachers and Trainers + Team Building Activity Guides.

This book belongs to

_____

I am an Earth Warrior!

I promise to protect the environment and will make sure to help mom and dad and the whole community in preserving our only home, **Earth**.

Thumbmark for the Earth!

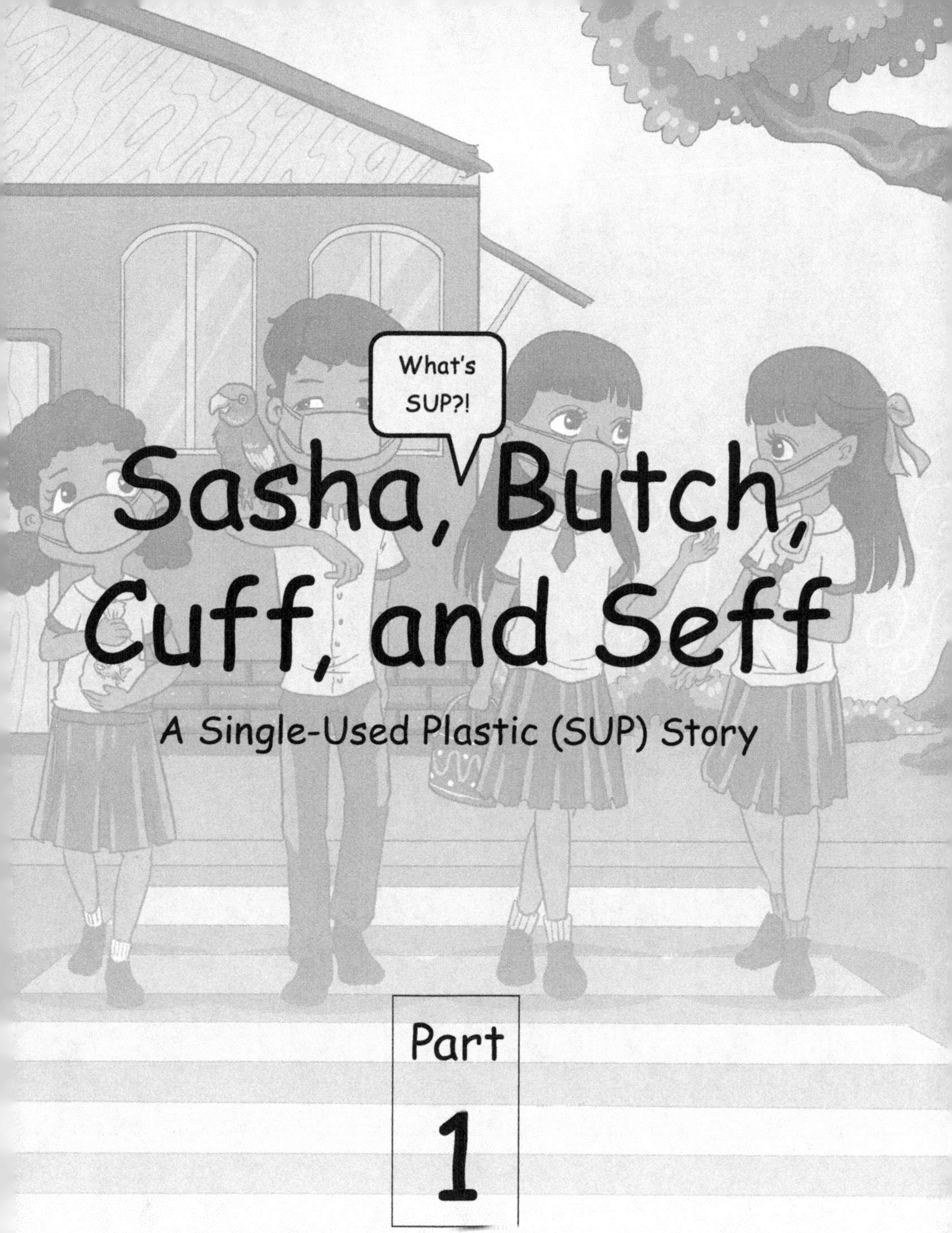

Sasha, Butch, Cuff, and Seff

A Single-Used Plastic (SUP) Story

Part 1

"Pet Day"

It is 7:00 in the morning and the heat of the sun is hurting. Sasha, Butch, Cuff, and Seff are preparing for school; Sasha and Butch are in 5th Grade while Cuff and Seff are in their 3rd. They are the top of their classes. Having brilliant minds, they excel in science, mathematics, arts, and literature, have proven their worth in this prestigious island school despite poverty.

Everyone was excited! They woke-up early and head to school quickly. They were fetched by Uncle Tonio and dropped them across the school. Sasha, Butch, Cuff and Seff are crossing the street; they are all wearing dust masks because of the recent forest fire near the school, cause by "kaingin" or bush clearing in preparation for the planting season.

In this volcanic island village of Camiguin, life is simple, coconut palms are everywhere, bird's chirping, cow's mooing, and the "tik tak, tik tak" sound from the horse carriage can be heard from afar, a provincial life it is.

Today is a big day, it's their "Pet Day" Presentation at School. The students will showcase their favorite pets in class.

Sasha brought her pet fish in a small plastic container, Butch has his parrot, which he named Chip, and Cuff & Seff brought pale and shovel with them and wanted to surprise everyone with their pet-peeking in the sand.

Sasha jumped-in when Teacher Nina called her name. Clearly, she's very excited and ready to present!

Sasha:

Good Morning Teacher Nina! Good Morning Classmates!

This is Bilbo! My pet goldfish,
My dad gave him to me, as my birthday wish,
Bilbo eats anything he sees,
We feed him daily, to keep him away from diseases

Bilbo loves to play,
He never missed the fun every day,
He makes me happy in any way!
He swims fast and also sway.

I love Bilbo so much,
I'm wearing an orange dress so we can match.
Promise Bilbo, I'll be at watch!
And take care of you, and catch that pussycat.

Sasha was applauded by her classmates, received a great feedback and a three stars from her Teacher Nina.

Teacher Nina got Butch's attention. Butch was asleep; he was tired from sleeping late last night.

Butch:

Hi Teacher Nina! Hi Friends!

Meet my pet "Chip",
She's lovely and sings at chirp!
We rescued her from a poacher,
I'm just happy she's now away from danger.

She doesn't like my Uncle Gary,
I think he makes her wary,
She called him ugly,
Uncle said she's maybe envy.

One day she escaped from her cage,
I was outraged,
Good thing she came back,
And felt the love she gave back!

Butch received great feedback for his presentation and also three stars from her Teacher Nina.

Cuff and Seff couldn't wait they raised their hands to present next. Teacher Nina was amazed! Called them to present, instead

Cuff and Seff:

Good Morning Everyone!

We have here our pet,
They are hidden on this pit
Can you guess it right?
Never take fright!

Seff slowly move the shovel,
Revealing a shell and claw in ravel,
Everyone was at awe,
When they see it crawls?

Hermit Crab was undeniably shy,
They hide when you touch them, Sly (friend),
But be careful they might bite your finger,
So never linger.

Butch received great feedback for his presentation and also three stars from her Teacher Nina.

Everyone was really happy with their presentation. Teacher Nina commended everyone for their effort and lively presentation.

"Getting to Know Sasha, Butch, Cuff and Seff"

Sasha

A petite girl with a brown complexion and a beautiful wide eye, kinky hair, her chubby chicks and coupled with a bubbly personality. She is the most loved in the group and a certified genius in literature and math.

Sasha loved her hair so much and wants it bouncy all the time. For her, it's like a crown she wears every day.

Butch

A 10-year old boy; he has wavy hair, a slanted eye, with fair complexion and a notable mole in his left chick which characterizes a typical Asian boy.

Butch has a pet parrot named, "Chip". A green native parrot with yellowish beck from the virgin forest of the Island of the Bohol.

"Cuff and Seff"

Cuff and Seff are twins with big round eyes, long hair with fairy-like ear, and a pointed one. They're lively and bubbly at the same time.

They love to play sands, they picked hermit crabs from a walking distant shore to play.

Glengyl Onga Umali

"Earth Warrior"

One day, Sasha, Butch, Cuff, and Seff went to a community coastal clean-up drive in the nearby surfing community of Siargao. Initiated by the Island government, non-government organization and people's organization in the area.

All of them were very excited to see their teachers, classmate, and families on the said activity. Each of them brought their garbage bags and hundreds of volunteers came to help and share their time for the clean-up drive.

Prrrrtttttttttt!!!!

As the sound of whistle echoed across, everyone heard it, which signals that the activity will start soon. A brown big guy with undercut hair introduces himself as the Earth Warrior, wearing a costume made by recyclable materials such as Plastic cups, woven plastic clothes, and everyone was amazed!

Shouting! Earth Warrior!!! Earth Warrior!!

Good Morning Earth Warriors! Let the games begin!

Earth Warrior: Let's start "The "Bring Me" Game!"

Who can bring me a shampoo sachet?

Sasha runs fast, she got her sachet from her pocket,

Earth Warrior! here it is! Sasha said.

"All right", thank you, Sasha!

Earth Warrior: Who can find a cigarette filter? Please don't forget to use your gloves when picking, okay?

Butch runs towards his brother and took the cigarette he put-off and gave it to Earth Warrior.

Earth Warrior, here it is! Butch said.

"All right", thank you, Butch!

Earth Warrior: Who can bring me Plastic cups or straws?

Good thing Cuff and Seff, just finish their drink, run towards Earth Warrior and gave the cups and straw Earth Warrior, here it is! Cuff and Seff said.

"All right", thank you!!

"The Sad Truth"

Earth Warrior commended Sasha, Butch, Cuff, and Seff for being so quick and responsive on his calls for the item asks.

You might have wondered I ask for these three things, it's empty, used and neglected, do you know that these items I am holding in my hands plays a significant role in destroying our planet?

Everyone was shocked and speechless, Earth Warrior continued, this Shampoo Sachet takes 400 years to decompose, the cigarette butt on the other hands need 200-300 years and the most culprit of all these utensils, cups and straw will take 100 to 1000 years to decompose. Imagine how long we have been using these single-used plastics.

Now, let's see how these small things destroyed and will continue to destroy our planet. Earth Warrior played a video of single-use plastics destroying the very core of the planet from plastics cups, tires, and clothes and waste we throw everywhere else.

Dumped, neglected absorbed and consumed by the birds, fishes and almost all living creatures vanished because of perpetual use of single-use plastics. Everyone shed tears and were sad. Sasha, Butch, Cuff, and Seff thought of their pets and cried.

From now on, let's protect our environment by following the 3R's Reuse, Reduce, Recycle and we shall declare an all-out-war on waste, especially the single-use plastics. Earth Warrior sent flyers and information sheets to the community

The End

Activity 1

Group yourselves to five (5) and discuss the things you've learn in the story.

Let us know below, what you've learned about "Sasha, Butch, Cuff and Seff" Story. Give us your insights and share it in this group.

1. List five (5) things you've learned about the story?
2. Is it really important to be concerned about single use plastics?
3. What help can you give to the community to reduce the use of single use plastics?
4. Who among the characters you like the most and why?

1. List five (5) things you've learned about the story?

   _____

   _____

   _____

   _____

   _____

   _____

   _____

   _____

   _____

   _____

   _____

   _____

   _____

   _____

   _____

   _____

   _____

   _____

2. Can you identify the characters bad practices contributing to the use of single use plastics?

_____

_____

_____

_____

_____

_____

_____

_____

_____

_____

_____

_____

_____

_____

_____

_____

3. What help can you give to the community to reduce the use of single use plastics?

4. Who among the characters you like the most and why?

_____

_____

_____

_____

_____

_____

_____

_____

_____

_____

_____

_____

_____

_____

_____

_____

_____

_____

Extra Sheet of Paper

Sasha, Butch, Cuff and Seff

Extra Sheet of Paper

_____

_____

_____

_____

_____

_____

_____

_____

_____

_____

_____

_____

_____

_____

_____

_____

_____

_____

_____

Extra Sheet of Paper

Sasha, Butch, Cuff and Seff

Extra Sheet of Paper

_____

_____

_____

_____

_____

_____

_____

_____

_____

_____

_____

_____

_____

_____

_____

_____

_____

_____

Extra Sheet of Paper

Sasha, Butch, Cuff and Seff

Extra Sheet of Paper

_____

_____

_____

_____

_____

_____

_____

_____

_____

_____

_____

_____

_____

_____

_____

_____

_____

_____

Extra Sheet of Paper

Sasha, Butch, Cuff and Seff

Extra Sheet of Paper

_____

_____

_____

_____

_____

_____

_____

_____

_____

_____

_____

_____

_____

_____

_____

_____

_____

_____

_____

Extra Sheet of Paper

Extra Sheet of Paper

Extra Sheet of Paper

Sasha, Butch, Cuff and Seff

Extra Sheet of Paper

_____

_____

_____

_____

_____

_____

_____

_____

_____

_____

_____

_____

_____

_____

_____

_____

_____

_____

_____

Extra Sheet of Paper

Sasha, Butch, Cuff and Seff

Extra Sheet of Paper

_____

_____

_____

_____

_____

_____

_____

_____

_____

_____

_____

_____

_____

_____

_____

_____

_____

_____

_____

Extra Sheet of Paper

Sasha, Butch, Cuff and Seff

Extra Sheet of Paper

_____

_____

_____

_____

_____

_____

_____

_____

_____

_____

_____

_____

_____

_____

_____

_____

_____

_____

Extra Sheet of Paper

_____

_____

_____

_____

_____

_____

_____

_____

_____

_____

_____

_____

_____

_____

_____

_____

_____

_____

_____

Sasha, Butch, Cuff and Seff

Extra Sheet of Paper

_____

_____

_____

_____

_____

_____

_____

_____

_____

_____

_____

_____

_____

_____

_____

_____

_____

_____

_____

Extra Sheet of Paper

Sasha, Butch, Cuff and Seff

Extra Sheet of Paper

_____

_____

_____

_____

Extra Sheet of Paper

Sasha, Butch, Cuff and Seff

Extra Sheet of Paper

_____

_____

_____

_____

_____

_____

_____

_____

_____

_____

_____

_____

_____

_____

_____

_____

_____

_____

_____

Extra Sheet of Paper

_____

_____

_____

_____

_____

_____

_____

_____

_____

_____

_____

_____

_____

_____

_____

_____

_____

_____

_____

_____

Sasha, Butch, Cuff and Seff

Extra Sheet of Paper

_____

_____

_____

_____

_____

_____

_____

_____

_____

_____

_____

_____

_____

_____

_____

_____

_____

_____

Extra Sheet of Paper

Sasha, Butch, Cuff and Seff

Extra Sheet of Paper

_____

_____

_____

_____

_____

_____

_____

_____

_____

_____

_____

_____

_____

_____

_____

_____

_____

_____

Extra Sheet of Paper

_____

_____

_____

_____

_____

_____

_____

_____

_____

_____

_____

_____

_____

_____

_____

_____

_____

_____

_____

_____

Sasha, Butch, Cuff and Seff

Extra Sheet of Paper

_____

_____

_____

_____

_____

_____

_____

_____

_____

_____

_____

_____

_____

_____

_____

_____

_____

_____

Extra Sheet of Paper

Extra Sheet of Paper

The

ABC

The ABC of Single Use Plastics
And Other Materials

Part
2

There are different kinds of plastic in the world. Through our Scientist's discoveries and Tinkers' greatest inventions, we can combine plastics with other materials such as rubber, metal, or glass, thereby prolonging its shelf life.

Now! Let's discover the compositions of plastics, we used at home and determine how long will it decompose or reintegrate into the environment. First Let's define single use plastic or commonly known as SUP. What is single use plastic?

Single used plastics are commercially produce goods that can be sold and found any where and every where we go. and with the word "Single-Used", this things can only be used once and people throw them away.

In the advent of technology (manufacturing products) coupled with extreme commercialism (consumption), most of us tend to buy things without considering its environmental impact.

Commercialism is the concept of buying and maximizing profits not because it's a need but more often, these are wants. Needs are necessities that one cannot live without. Wants, on the other hand, is a desire to have or possess something.

In some societies, wants can be considered as similar to emotional desires, which can be understood further scientifically through the disciplines of psychology or sociology.

In the eyes of a kid, everything will always be right, empowering them with the right knowledge and awareness towards environmental protection, our chance for a better start in a world were forest degradation and massive pollution which both human and animals' lives are at stake. We can still revert this by making livable and sustainable planet.

TYPES OF RUBBER
1. Natural Rubber (Polyisoprene)
2. SBR (Styrene-Butadiene-Rubber)
3. EPDM (EPDM ETHYLENE PROPYLENE)
4. Butyl Rubber.
5. Polyurethane (AU, EU)
6. Neoprene CR (Polychloroprene)
7. Hydrogenated Nitrile (Hnbr Hsn)
8. HYPALON Chlorosulphonated Polyethylene (CSM)

TYPES OF PLASTICS
1. Acrylic or Polymethyl Methacrylate (PMMA) ...
2. Polycarbonate (PC) ...
3. Polyethylene (PE) ...
4. Polypropylene (PP) ...
5. Polyethylene Terephthalate (PETE or PET) ...
6. Polyvinyl Chloride (PVC) ...
7. Acrylonitrile-Butadiene-Styrene (ABS)

PLASTIC – GLASS COATING
1. Acrylic and Polycarbonate

PLASTIC – PAPER COATING
1. Polyethylene (LDPE)
2. Frozen food cartons

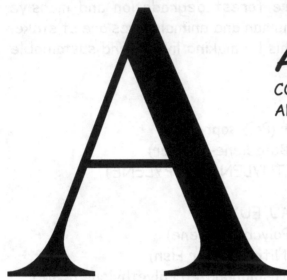

Adhesives
COMPOSITION OF ADHESIVE TAPES
1. Plastic
2. Metal

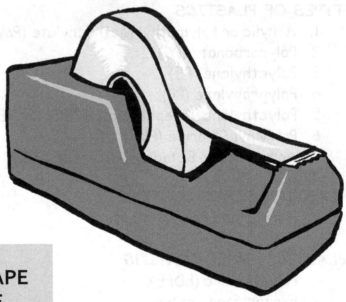

ADHESIVE TAPE
WILL TAKE

45

YEARS TO
DECOMPOSE

COLOR ME

Balloons
TYPES OF RUBBER
1. Plastic
2. Rubber

BALLOONS
WILL TAKE

04

YEARS TO
DECOMPOSE

C

Cigarette
Filter

CIGARETTES
WILL TAKE

12

YEARS TO
DECOMPOSE

COLOR ME

Diaper

COMPOSITION OF
DIAPERS

1. Plastic
2. Rubber
3. Cotton

COLOR ME

DIAPERS
WILL TAKE

500

YEARS TO
DECOMPOSE

Ear Swabs

COMPOSITION OF
EAR SWABS
1. Plastic
2. Cotton

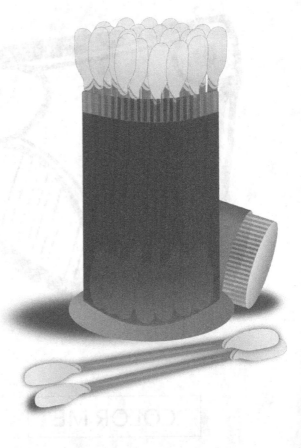

EAR SWABS
WILL TAKE

3

MONTHS TO
DECOMPOSE

Food Container

TYPES OF FOOD CONTAINERS

1. Styrofoam
2. Paper
3. Plastic

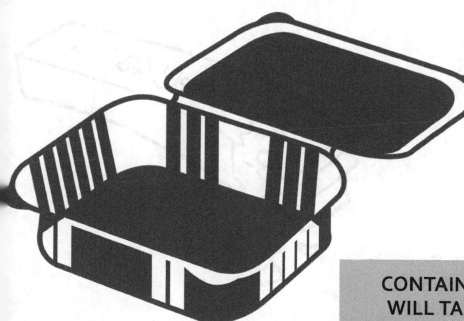

CONTAINER
WILL TAKE

450

YEARS TO
DECOMPOSE

G

Gum
COMPOSITION OF GUMS
1. Rubber
2. Plastic

GUMS WILL TAKE

50

YEARS TO DECOMPOSE

COLOR ME

Hair Brush

COMPOSITION OF
HAIR BRUSH

1. Plastic
2. Rubber

HAIR BRUSH
WILL TAKE

200

YEARS TO
DECOMPOSE

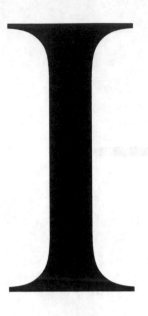

Insecticide

COMPOSITION OF
INSECTICIDES

1. Plastic
2. Metal
3. Aluminum/Tin Metal

AEROSOL CANS
WILL TAKE

200

YEARS TO
DECOMPOSE

COLOR ME

Jar (Glass)

COMPOSITION OF JARS

1. Glass
2. Plastic
3. Rubber

J

COLOR ME

K

Knitting Yarn

COMPOSITION OF YARNS
1. Cloth
2. Nylon

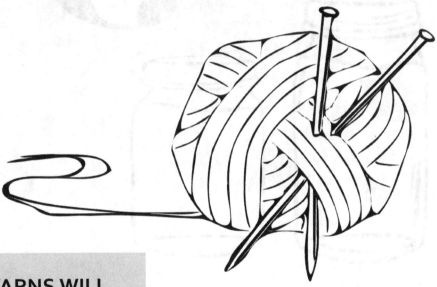

YARNS WILL TAKE

5

YEARS TO DECOMPOSE

COLOR ME

LED Bulb

COMPOSITION OF BULBS
1. Glass
2. Plastic
3. Metal

L

COLOR ME

LED BULB
WILL TAKE

FOREVER

TO DECOMPOSE

M

Milk

COMPOSITION OF
TETRA PACK
1. Paper
2. Plastic

TETRA PACK
WILL TAKE UP TO

05

YEARS TO
DECOMPOSE

COLOR ME

Net
COMPOSITION OF
FISH NET
1. Nylon
2. Plastic

COLOR ME

FISH NET
WILL TAKE

600

YEARS TO
DECOMPOSE

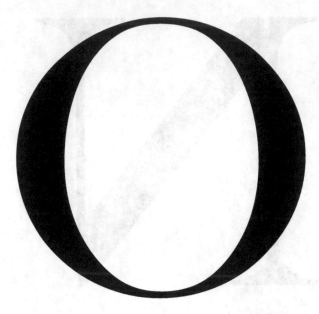

O

ORNAMENTAL
Flowers
COMPOSITION OF
ORNAMENTAL FLOWERS
1. Plastic
2. Rubber

**ORNAMENTAL
FLOWERS WILL TAKE**

450

**YEARS TO
DECOMPOSE**

Plastic Bottle
COMPOSITION OF PLASTIC
BAGS.
1. Paper
2. Plastic
3. Cellophane

PLASTIC BOTTLE
WILL TAKE

450

YEARS TO
DECOMPOSE

Quiver
COMPOSITION OF
QUIVER TOYS.
1. Plastic
2. Rubber
3. Metal

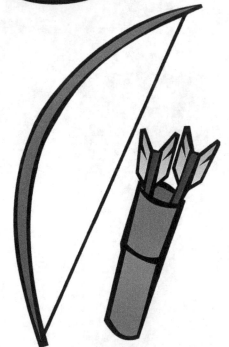

QUIVER TOYS
WILL TAKE

400

YEARS TO
DECOMPOSE

COLOR ME

R

Rubber Ducky

COMPOSITION OF RUBBER
DUCKIES.

1. Rubber
2. Plastic

**RUBBER DUCKY
WILL TAKE**

80

**YEARS TO
DECOMPOSE**

COLOR ME

Sweet Candies
COMPOSITION OF CANDY WRAPPERS
1. Plastic
2. Paper

WRAPPER WILL TAKE

400

YEARS TO DECOMPOSE

COLOR ME

Tires

COMPOSITION OF
TIRES

1. Plastic
2. Rubber
3. Metal

T

TIRES
WILL TAKE

80

YEARS TO
DECOMPOSE

Utensils
COMPOSITION OF UTENSILS
1. Plastic
2. Metal

UTENSILS
WILL TAKE

100

TO 1000 YEARS
TO DECOMPOSE

Vinyl

COMPOSITION OF VINYL

1. Plastic
2. Rubber
3. Vinyl

VINYL
WILL TAKE

450

YEARS TO
DECOMPOSE

W

Wet Tissue

COMPOSITION OF
WATER BOTTLE

1. Plastic
2. Rubber
3. Metal
4. Glass

WET TISSUE
WILL TAKE

100

YEARS TO
DECOMPOSE

COLOR ME

X-Ray

COMPOSITION OF
X-RAY

1. Plastic

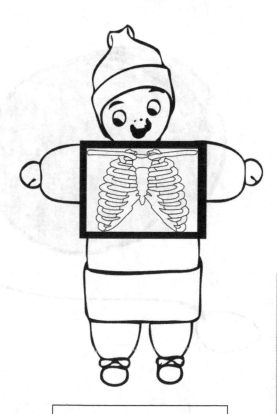

COLOR ME

X-RAY FILM
WILL TAKE

20

YEARS TO
DECOMPOSE

Yoyo
COMPOSITION OF YOYO
1. Plastic
2. Thread
3. Rubber

YOYO
WILL TAKE

450

YEARS TO
DECOMPOSE

COLOR ME

Zipper

COMPOSITION OF ZIPPERS

1. Plastic
2. Metal

Activity 2

Let us know what you've learned in "Single-Used Plastics Alphabet". Give us your insights and share it here.

Group yourself to five (5) and discuss about all the things that you've learn in the ABCs. Using the following guide, share your discovery!

1. List five (5) things you used at home that you consider "Single Use" plastics.
2. Using the Life Cycle of "SUP" on the alphabet, when do you think your things you listed will decompose?
3. Based on your own words. What can you do to help the environment?
4. Is it important to help save the planet as a family? If Yes, Share your story/if No, why?

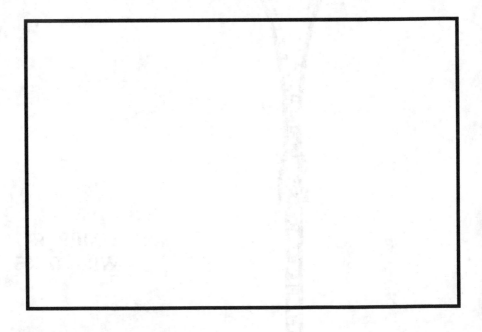

1. List five (5) things you used at home, that you consider "Single Use" plastics.

_____

_____

_____

_____

2. Using the Life Cycle of "SUP" on the alphabet, when do you think your things you listed will decompose?

_____

_____

_____

_____

_____

_____

_____

_____

_____

_____

_____

_____

_____

_____

_____

_____

3. Based on your own words. What can you do to help the environment?

_____

_____

_____

_____

_____

_____

_____

_____

_____

_____

_____

_____

_____

_____

_____

_____

4. Is it important to help save the planet as a family? If Yes, Share your story/if No, why?

_____

_____

_____

_____

_____

_____

_____

_____

_____

_____

_____

_____

_____

_____

_____

_____

Extra Sheet of Paper

Sasha, Butch, Cuff and Seff

Extra Sheet of Paper

_____

_____

_____

_____

_____

_____

_____

_____

_____

_____

_____

_____

_____

_____

_____

_____

_____

_____

Extra Sheet of Paper

_____

_____

_____

_____

_____

_____

_____

_____

_____

_____

_____

_____

_____

_____

_____

_____

_____

_____

_____

Sasha, Butch, Cuff and Seff

Extra Sheet of Paper

_____

_____

_____

_____

_____

_____

_____

_____

_____

_____

_____

_____

_____

_____

_____

_____

_____

_____

_____

Extra Sheet of Paper

_____

_____

_____

_____

_____

_____

_____

_____

_____

_____

_____

_____

_____

_____

_____

_____

_____

_____

_____

_____

Extra Sheet of Paper

Extra Sheet of Paper

Sasha, Butch, Cuff and Seff

Extra Sheet of Paper

Extra Sheet of Paper

Extra Sheet of Paper

_____

_____

_____

_____

_____

_____

_____

_____

_____

_____

_____

_____

_____

_____

_____

_____

_____

_____

Extra Sheet of Paper

_____

_____

_____

_____

_____

_____

_____

_____

_____

_____

_____

_____

_____

_____

_____

_____

_____

_____

_____

Sasha, Butch, Cuff and Seff

Extra Sheet of Paper

_____

_____

_____

_____

_____

_____

_____

_____

_____

_____

_____

_____

_____

_____

_____

_____

_____

Extra Sheet of Paper

Extra Sheet of Paper

_____

_____

_____

_____

_____

_____

_____

_____

_____

_____

_____

_____

_____

_____

_____

_____

_____

_____

_____

Extra Sheet of Paper

Extra Sheet of Paper

_____

_____

_____

_____

_____

_____

_____

_____

_____

_____

_____

_____

_____

_____

_____

_____

_____

_____

_____

Extra Sheet of Paper

Sasha, Butch, Cuff and Seff

Extra Sheet of Paper

_____

_____

_____

_____

_____

_____

_____

_____

_____

_____

_____

_____

_____

_____

_____

_____

_____

_____

_____

Extra Sheet of Paper

_____

_____

_____

_____

_____

_____

_____

_____

_____

_____

_____

_____

_____

_____

_____

_____

_____

_____

_____

_____

Extra Sheet of Paper

_____

_____

_____

_____

_____

_____

_____

_____

_____

_____

_____

_____

_____

_____

_____

_____

_____

_____

_____

Extra Sheet of Paper

Sasha, Butch, Cuff and Seff

Extra Sheet of Paper

_____

_____

_____

_____

_____

_____

_____

_____

_____

_____

_____

_____

_____

_____

_____

_____

_____

_____

Extra Sheet of Paper

Sasha, Butch, Cuff and Seff

Extra Sheet of Paper

Extra Sheet of Paper

_____

_____

_____

_____

_____

_____

_____

_____

_____

_____

_____

_____

_____

_____

_____

_____

_____

_____

_____

_____

Extra Sheet of Paper

_____

_____

_____

_____

_____

_____

_____

_____

_____

_____

_____

_____

_____

_____

_____

_____

_____

_____

Extra Sheet of Paper

Sasha, Butch, Cuff and Seff

Extra Sheet of Paper

_____

_____

_____

_____

_____

_____

_____

_____

_____

_____

_____

_____

_____

_____

_____

_____

_____

_____

_____

Extra Sheet of Paper

Be an Earth Warrior!

Ocean and Corals Activity Book

Glengyl Onga Umali

Coral Reefs...

...for health, for wealth, for life
Did you know...?

Coral reefs can be found in all tropical areas of the world. Corals can also be found in deep cold oceans.

Most corals grow very, very slowly... it can take hundreds to thousands of years for a reef to form.

Coral reefs can be large or small. The Great Barrier Reef in Australia is over 1,200 miles long.

Coral reefs are some of the oldest ecosystems on the planet.

Color Me!

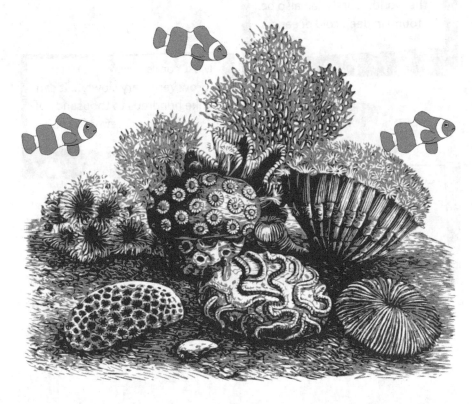

There are thousands of species of coral, some named for their colors, others named for their shapes. In this picture are a brain coral, a staghorn coral, and a sea fan.
Can you guess which one is which?

Connect the dots!

Sea Stars have a strange way of eating. When they find something tasty, they can push their stomachs outside of their body and digest their food right there! Once they're finished, they pull their stomach back inside... until the next meal.

Color Me!

Coral animals (polyps) are often protected by hard skeletons that form many different shapes. Large areas of coral are called coral reefs, and these occur in warm shallow seas.

Word Search
Can you find these coral words?

S	A	E	Z	O	O	P	L	A	N	K	T	O	N	R
T	O	C	O	R	A	L	R	E	E	F	E	O	R	O
O	K	P	O	L	Y	P	R	D	E	A	T	S	A	A
N	O	L	X	O	T	L	C	G	A	M	L	N	R	O
Y	S	P	A	W	N	I	N	G	N	S	L	T	T	M
S	M	T	N	E	M	A	T	O	C	Y	S	T	N	N
P	H	O	T	O	S	Y	N	T	H	E	S	I	S	E
A	A	T	H	O	R	S	E	L	K	H	O	R	N	B
W	T	A	E	N	E	E	I	S	S	A	F	N	A	A
N	O	B	L	E	A	C	H	I	N	G	T	L	B	R
I	L	L	L	N	T	E	N	E	Z	R	C	G	R	R
N	L	E	A	N	E	M	O	N	E	S	O	P	A	I
G	E	T	E	M	P	E	R	A	T	U	R	E	I	E
D	I	V	E	R	S	E	A	N	I	M	A	L	N	R
D	I	V	E	R	S	E	A	F	A	N	L	R	A	L

Words are found down and across:

Zooxanthellae   Polyp   Nematocyst   Diverse
Coral Reef   Photosynthesis   Elkhorn   Bleaching
Anemone   Animal   Table   Temperature
Zooplankton   Stony   Spawning   Brain
Soft coral   Sea fan   Atoll   Barrier

Color Me!

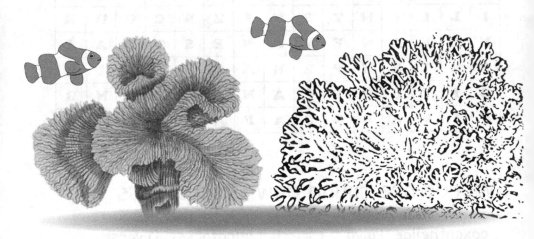

Several species of fish spend part or all of their lives in association with sea anemones. The clownfish does not stray far from its anemone. This lets the fish avoid being eaten by other fish by hiding in the anemone's stinging tentacles. Clownfish have a special mucus coating that protects them from the anemone's stinging cells.

A-Maze Me

Help Sasha, Butch, Cuff and Seff collecting single-used plastics and put it on the recycling bin,

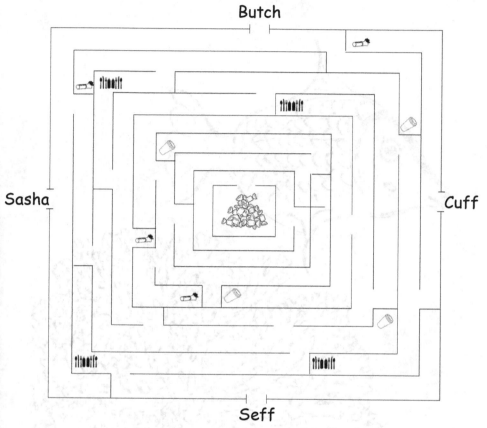

Butch

Sasha

Cuff

Seff

How many SUP were they able to collect?

Sasha: _____

Butch: _____

Cuff: _____

Seff: _____

Helper Fish

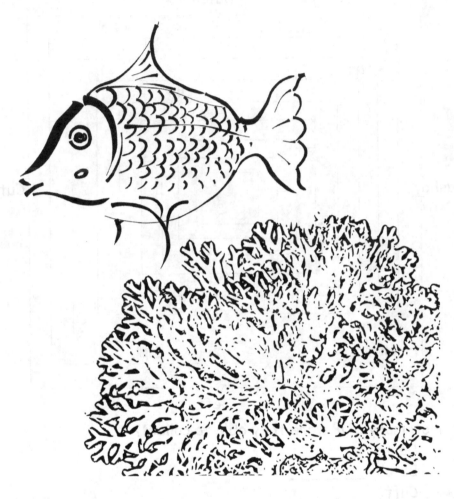

Parrotfish are named for their bright colors and strong beak-like jaws, used to bite off chunks of coral. They like to eat the plants (algae) that grow on corals.

Parrotfish have a special grinding plate in their throat which they use to grind up the coral's hard skeleton.

When they are finished, all that is left is fine sand.

Glengyl Onga Umali

Connect the dots

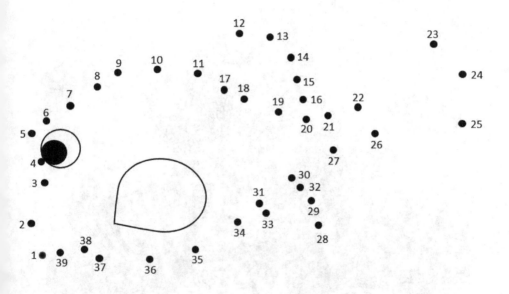

Boxfish are covered with a bad-tasting slime, which protects them from being eaten.

City of Life

A reef is like a busy city. More creatures live on coral reefs than in any other habitat in the ocean. Each animal and plant on or around the reef has a job to keep the ecosystem healthy. How many different animals can you count on this reef?

Word Search

Can you find these coral reef words?

C	L	Y	H	L	R	B	F	N	L	P	M	F	W	I
R	E	E	F	S	H	A	R	K	P	N	P	O	O	B
A	H	L	D	H	G	R	G	H	D	W	G	O	R	D
B	I	L	H	M	O	R	A	Y	E	E	L	D	M	P
S	P	O	N	G	E	A	N	G	E	L	F	I	S	H
N	R	W	R	R	R	C	A	R	P	S	L	V	U	R
I	R	T	F	O	W	U	A	E	C	E	L	E	D	F
N	O	A	Y	T	A	D	T	L	O	A	H	R	S	A
L	Y	N	T	R	E	A	O	D	R	U	M	S	A	F
Y	W	G	L	O	B	A	L	W	A	R	M	I	N	G
G	R	O	U	P	E	R	L	E	L	C	A	T	Y	E
B	A	R	R	I	E	R	Y	R	S	H	S	Y	M	N
Y	S	W	E	C	F	R	I	N	G	I	N	G	A	A
A	S	W	R	A	M	W	A	O	I	N	Y	E	Y	B
J	E	W	E	L	R	Y	A	F	L	R	I	M	O	A

Words are found down and across.

FOOD
DIVERSITY
FRINGING
BARRIER
ATOLL
GLOBAL WARMING

MORAL EEL
REEF SHARK
CRABS
CORALS
YELLOW TANG
TROPICAL

ANGEL FISH
DEEP CORAL
SEA URCHIN
WORMS
WRASSE
SPONGE

BARRACUDA
GROUPER
DRUM
JEWELRY

Secret Code

Even if you live far from the ocean, your actions impact coral reefs around the world.

Find out how you can make a difference by decoding the secret message.

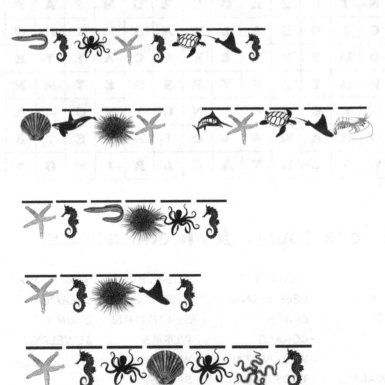

Word Search

It is estimated that 13 million pounds of litter are put into the ocean each year.*. This litter is generated by many sources, from boats and oil rigs on the water to picnickers, fisherman, and beachgoers along the shore, hidden below is a list of objects that have been discarded into our oceans. See if you can find them all.

N	B	A	B	I	H	O	S	E	A	T	M	R	G	E
E	G	U	T	A	C	A	N	C	E	W	E	L	L	A
K	L	R	C	R	L	A	R	N	R	N	O	U	A	R
T	O	A	P	K	C	L	G	D	I	A	K	M	S	T
R	V	D	O	A	E	N	O	A	H	W	T	B	S	H
A	E	I	D	W	I	T	T	O	A	A	M	E	B	W
S	H	O	E	H	D	N	G	R	N	L	T	R	O	A
H	S	W	S	B	O	T	T	L	E	C	A	P	T	R
B	K	I	P	C	T	S	J	B	U	R	G	Y	T	R
A	F	U	T	D	I	A	P	E	R	D	O	L	L	I
G	C	I	G	A	R	E	T	T	E	U	T	P	E	O
W	A	N	X	O	E	U	O	H	B	A	S	N	E	R
B	F	I	S	H	I	N	G	L	I	N	E	H	M	S
G	I	L	A	T	O	Y	M	A	R	Y	F	G	M	T
Y	O	Y	O	K	U	Y	A	G	B	O	Y	S	G	M

BAIT CONTAINER	CRATE	FISHING NET	LUMBER	SHOE
BALLOON	CUP	GLASS BOTTLE	PAINT BRUSH	SODA CAN
BUCKET	DIAPER	GLOVE	RADIO	STRAW
BUOY	DOLL	HARD HAT	ROPE	TIRE
CIGARETTE	FISHING LINE	HOSE	RUG	TRASH BAG

MAZE

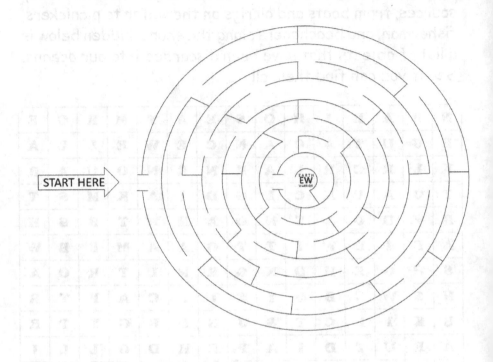

START HERE

Be an Earth Warrior! Get the magical power at the very core of your belief and love for the environment!

Glengyl Onga Umali

What's Wrong in this Picture?

What's Wrong in this Picture?

Glengyl Onga Umali

What's Wrong in this Picture?

Sasha, Butch, Cuff and Seff

Express Your Creativity in Saving Earth Here!

Express Your Creativity in Saving Earth Here!

Sasha, Butch, Cuff and Seff

Express Your Creativity in Saving Earth Here!

Express Your Creativity in Saving Earth Here!

Sasha, Butch, Cuff and Seff

Express Your Creativity in Saving Earth Here!

Express Your Creativity in Saving Earth Here!

Sasha, Butch, Cuff and Seff

Express Your Creativity in Saving Earth Here!

Express Your Creativity in Saving Earth Here!

Express Your Creativity in Saving Earth Here!

Express Your Creativity in Saving Earth Here!

Express Your Creativity in Saving Earth Here!

Express Your Creativity in Saving Earth Here!

Express Your Creativity in Saving Earth Here!

Express Your Creativity in Saving Earth Here!

Express Your Creativity in Saving Earth Here!

Express Your Creativity in Saving Earth Here!

Sasha, Butch, Cuff and Seff

Express Your Creativity in Saving Earth Here!

Express Your Creativity in Saving Earth Here!

Sasha, Butch, Cuff and Seff

Express Your Creativity in Saving Earth Here!

Express Your Creativity in Saving Earth Here!

Express Your Creativity in Saving Earth Here!

Express Your Creativity in Saving Earth Here!

Sasha, Butch, Cuff and Seff

Express Your Creativity in Saving Earth Here!

Express Your Creativity in Saving Earth Here!

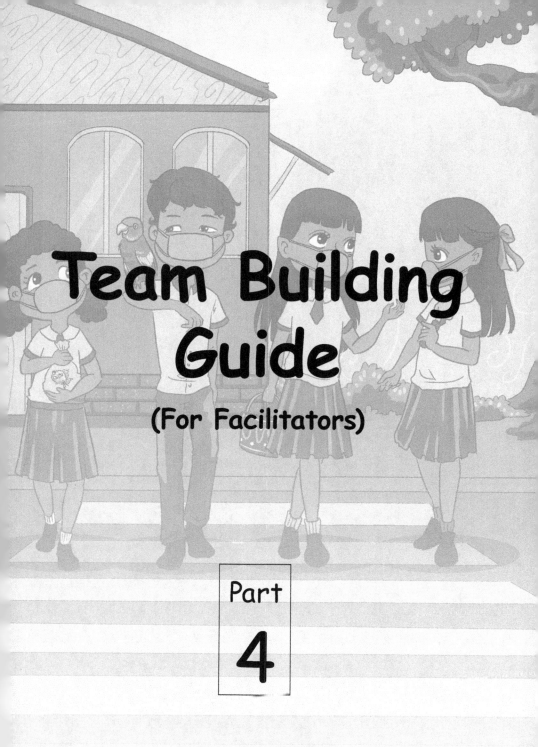

Team Building Guide

(For Facilitators)

Part

4

PROGRAM

Rationale:

Team building activity initiatives has always been considered in a group or an organization, driven by various issues that can trigger anytime, which concernis team workers, such as issues in performance, attitudes and relationships. Most often, it is also being thought as fun and enjoyable, where team players may maximize in order to unwind and break away from daily work routines. The team process may be integrated in the annual rest and recreation activity that somehow provides venue and mechanism of getting along with and expands the horizon of friendship to its greater heights that may give more opportunities for examination, reflection and growth.

Objective:

1) *Build a strong bond of connections by creating an atmosphere of dialogue through friendship building processes;*
2) *Maximize the free space of conquering fears, recollecting team efforts in the past and facing team goals and purpose for an effective understanding of a team-oriented environment;*
3) *Imbibe the spirit of 'One' that maybe strengthened of the belief on being 'All of Us' that not a single one can be better to it that leads the team to work effectively.*

Team Building Guide

Team Building can sometimes be strenuous to prepare, as to the games to play, lessons or challenges and key areas to target and depending on the organization area for improvement, we always consider the goals to achieve. Trust me it is not just any team-building activity would work, you have to make sure that it's in line with your goals and always aim for an unforgettable outcome for your team.

The usual team building that may happen in any setting are the R & R, Eat-out, and Open sessions, which does not establish organizational development that could correct behavior. If you want to make an on-point changes for your team! It's time to make a fun and exciting challenges which you can find here at this Team-Building Guide.

Here are the guide you can follow: Tweak, Edit or change it to any activity deemed important for your team and never set aside the dynamics and composition of the team especially when you do the grouping.

1. Grouping (Not about Color, Race or religion)
Divide the team to three or depending on the number of participants, make sure the strong, the strategist, the wise, the weak are well distributed. You cannot have one team that has all intelligent individual and strong it will only defeat the purpose of the team composition they will just dominate and undermine others. There is no fair game if that's the case.

2. Facilitator
Select a facilitator that can monitor progress step by step. Their job is to tally points gained each team. A facilitator will not give clue nor aid the team, it will be called cheating. They are there to cheer and move the team towards the goal and note every challenges to ponder at the end of the game.

3. Props

Prepare colored flags made out of cut "Gina Earth" Cloth. Each team should have their own color embedded with their own logo (a guide can be downloaded below) and materials needed for each activity. Need items may differ from the number of teams created.

4. Start the Game!

Guides available on the next pages

5. Processing

It is important to take each challenges and be able to discuss it at the end of the game. A forum is needed making sure the members and leaders settle each challenges.

a. Start by asking each experiences and integrate work ethics and key performance.
b. Camaraderie is crucial and needed to emphasize on each team-building activity. There is no I but we is appreciated in a team building.
c. Thank everyone for their efforts it would be good if a plaque of appreciation is available or sweets or freebies for the winning team and for the losers you can have them wash plates or clean their room or prepare food. It's up to you!

Sasha, Butch, Cuff and Seff

PROGRAM ACTIVITY GUIDE
Facilitator's Copy

Location: _____

1. _____
2. _____
3. _____
4. _____
5. _____
6. _____
7. _____
8. _____
9. _____
10. _____
11. _____
12. _____
13. _____
14. _____
15. _____
16. _____
17. _____
18. _____
19. _____
20. _____

Guest/Member Facilitator

1. _____
2. _____
3. _____

Notes:

_____
_____
_____
_____

Facilitator's Copy Page 1 Station 1
STATION ONE:

BIO-HAZARDS

Scenario:

A group of bad people planned to spread toxic chemicals in Camiguin Island. Its horrific goal is to cripple Island's economy and its tourist. As a member of the select Earth Warrior, you are all given a highly confidential mission and this is to transport toxic chemicals to safety in Station 2 Lab to neutralize it.

You are given protective thread and holding the container is highly forbidden and detrimental. Take all chemicals to the Lab and fill the specialized container with it until full. Be extra cautious any spill could threaten the island. Handle everything with care. (You are given 2 min to read and understand, non-compliance may deduct points)

Materials Needed:
1. 6 inches Garter
2. Colored Thread
3. 3 pcs tin can

Instructions:

From the starting point fill tin can with the toxic chemicals and transport it over to the second station, pour it gently in the empty bucket, don't touch the tin can, use the thread to that's provided then back, until the bucket is full.

Tip: Work as one, win as one. Strategies are highly encouraged.

Facilitator:
Encourage Team members; Cheer and applaud your team. Verify if task was done properly, you have the right to suspend and send them back to the start point when deceit and shortcuts occur.

STATION TWO:

CO2

Scenario:

Siargao's–PAG-ASA's Dr. Faith Umali have discovered the conversion of Carbon dioxide (CO2) to clean air both beneficial to our flora and fauna. Dr. Faith is in need of volunteer to generate high-quality CO2 from your team.

Specialized elastic containers are provided for your team. Inflate the rubberized container until full blown. Form one line with each container sandwiched on each member without holding it and walk your way together to Dr. Faith's Lab Station 3. **(You are given 2 min to read and understand, none-compliance may deduct points)**

Instructions:

Inflate balloon till full blown, form one line with each balloon sandwiched on each member without holding it and walk your way together onto the third station

Materials Needed:

1. BALLOON

Facilitator:

Encourage Team members; Cheer and applaud your team. Verify if task was done properly, you have the right to suspend and send them back to the start point when deceit and shortcuts occur.

185

Sasha, Butch, Cuff and Seff

STATION THREE:

YEPO ITATA

Scenario:
The Central Intelligence of Bohol Island (CIB) called the attention and requested help from our President. The Cultural Office of Siargao through the mandate given by the President, they have identified your team as the sole member of the Indigenous People to unify the People of Pangangan Island, Bohol to cast the unifying chant as clear and loud as possible. **(You are given 2 min to read and understand, none-compliance may deduct points)**

Instructions:
All for one, one for All, Sing and Act! The team will choose one member to act the YEPO ITATA; and the remaining members will SING it, once done the remaining member will then act the YEPO ITATA and the previously chosen member will sing it. Synchronization is very crucial.

Materials Needed:
1. Copies/Lyrics of Yepo Itata

Facilitator:
Encourage Team members; Cheer and applaud your team. Verify if task was done properly, you have the right to suspend and send them back to the start point when deceit and shortcuts occur.

STOP FOR

MINI GAME

BLOCK MEMBERS from heading to the fourth station and bearing the sign DETOUR. Have the team choose a box to perform the task. Ensure progress completion and tally minutes of execution.

Facilitator's Copy Page 3 Station 4
STATION FOUR

THE PROTOTYPE

Scenario:
Siargao's Tourism Board have planned to create a replica of the Eiffel Tower of Paris Earth Warriors are once again called for your skills.

To construct a tower as high as possible, by only using the available pasta sticks and marshmallows. Limited supply of materials are available. Pieces of spaghetti may be broken in desired length. **(You are given 2 min to read and understand, none-compliance may deduct points)**

Only the materials provided may be used.

Materials Needed:

1. Spaghetti sticks
2. Marshmallows

Facilitator:
Encourage Team members; Cheer and applaud your team. Verify if task was done properly, you have the right to suspend and send them back to the start point when deceit and shortcuts occur.

STATION FIVE

INVISIBILITY

Scenario:

You are on Skull Island, Earth Warrior were instructed to assess the situation and report it to the Bureau and in order to survive you have to act as one of the zombies. Three of the four members will wear blindfolds and one will serve as a guide, Identify a unique sound that you can use to call-out your team, make sure to identify the best call-out name to avoid confusion, make your team follow to the fifth station. **(You are given 2 min to read and understand, none-compliance may deduct points)**

NOTE: Before leaving, each team they must compose its own jingle and march towards the finish line and perform it. The Guide will make sure everyone's safety and the first one to arrive will be declared TEAM DON'S CHAMPION

Materials Needed:

1. Hood will serve as a blindfold

Facilitator:

Encourage Team members; Cheer and applaud your team. Verify if task was done properly, you have the right to suspend and send them back to the start point when deceit and shortcuts occur.

Facilitator's Notes

_____

_____

_____

_____

_____

_____

_____

_____

_____

_____

_____

_____

_____

_____

_____

_____

_____

_____

_____

_____

Facilitator's Notes

_____

_____

_____

_____

_____

_____

_____

_____

_____

_____

_____

_____

_____

_____

_____

_____

_____

_____

_____

Facilitator's Notes

Facilitator's Notes

_____

_____

_____

_____

_____

_____

_____

_____

_____

_____

_____

_____

_____

_____

_____

_____

_____

_____

_____

Facilitator's Notes

_____

_____

_____

_____

_____

_____

_____

_____

_____

_____

_____

_____

_____

_____

_____

_____

_____

_____

_____

_____

Facilitator's Notes

_____

_____

_____

_____

_____

_____

_____

_____

_____

_____

_____

_____

_____

_____

_____

_____

_____

_____

Facilitator's Notes

_____

_____

_____

_____

_____

_____

_____

_____

_____

_____

_____

_____

_____

_____

_____

_____

_____

_____

_____

_____

_____

Facilitator's Notes

_____

_____

_____

_____

_____

_____

_____

_____

_____

_____

_____

_____

_____

_____

_____

_____

_____

_____

_____

Facilitator's Notes

_____

_____

_____

_____

_____

_____

_____

_____

_____

_____

_____

_____

_____

_____

_____

_____

_____

_____

_____

_____

_____

Facilitator's Notes

_____

_____

_____

_____

_____

_____

_____

_____

_____

_____

_____

_____

_____

_____

_____

_____

_____

Facilitator's Notes

_____

_____

_____

_____

_____

_____

_____

_____

_____

_____

_____

_____

_____

_____

_____

_____

_____

_____

_____

_____

_____

Facilitator's Notes

_____

_____

_____

_____

_____

_____

_____

_____

_____

_____

_____

_____

_____

_____

_____

_____

_____

_____

_____

_____

Facilitator's Notes

_____

_____

_____

_____

_____

_____

_____

_____

_____

_____

_____

_____

_____

_____

_____

_____

_____

_____

_____

_____

Facilitator's Notes

_____

_____

_____

_____

_____

_____

_____

_____

_____

_____

_____

_____

_____

_____

_____

_____

_____

_____

_____

_____

Facilitator's Notes

_____

_____

_____

_____

_____

_____

_____

_____

_____

_____

_____

_____

_____

_____

_____

_____

_____

_____

_____

_____

_____

Facilitator's Notes

_____

_____

_____

_____

_____

_____

_____

_____

_____

_____

_____

_____

_____

_____

_____

_____

_____

_____

_____

Facilitator's Notes

_____

_____

_____

_____

_____

_____

_____

_____

_____

_____

_____

_____

_____

_____

_____

_____

_____

_____

_____

_____

Facilitator's Notes

_____

_____

_____

_____

_____

_____

_____

_____

_____

_____

_____

_____

_____

_____

_____

_____

_____

_____

_____

Facilitator's Notes

_____

_____

_____

_____

_____

_____

_____

_____

_____

_____

_____

_____

_____

_____

_____

_____

_____

_____

_____

_____

Facilitator's Notes

_____

_____

_____

_____

_____

_____

_____

_____

_____

_____

_____

_____

_____

_____

_____

_____

_____

_____

Facilitator's Notes

_____

_____

_____

_____

_____

_____

_____

_____

_____

_____

_____

_____

_____

_____

_____

_____

_____

_____

_____

_____

_____

Sasha, Butch, Cuff and Seff

Facilitator's Notes

_____

_____

_____

_____

_____

_____

_____

_____

_____

_____

_____

_____

_____

_____

_____

_____

_____

_____

Facilitator's Notes

_____

_____

_____

_____

_____

_____

_____

_____

_____

_____

_____

_____

_____

_____

_____

_____

_____

_____

_____

_____

Facilitator's Notes

_____

_____

_____

_____

_____

_____

_____

_____

_____

_____

_____

_____

_____

_____

_____

_____

_____

_____

Facilitator's Notes

_____

_____

_____

_____

_____

_____

_____

_____

_____

_____

_____

_____

_____

_____

_____

_____

_____

_____

_____

_____

_____

Facilitator's Notes

_____

_____

_____

_____

_____

_____

_____

_____

_____

_____

_____

_____

_____

_____

_____

_____

_____

_____

_____

_____

Facilitator's Notes

_____

_____

_____

_____

_____

_____

_____

_____

_____

_____

_____

_____

_____

_____

_____

_____

_____

_____

_____

Let's aim for Plastic Free Communities!

References

Protecting Our Oceans Activity Book
The National Oceanic and Atmospheric Administration
1401 Constitution Avenue
Washington DC 20230 www.noaa.gov ; www.marinedebris.noaa.gov ; www.sanctuarues.noaa.gov

Coral Reef Coloring Book
The National Oceanic and Atmospheric Administration
1401 Constitution Avenue
Washington DC 20230 www.noaa.gov; http://coastalscience.noaa.gov/education

What are the Different Types of Plastic?
by Alyssa Mertes Published: June 14th, 2019
724 North Highland Avenue, Aurora, Illinois 60506
info@qualitylogoproducts.com

Illustration Reference Downloaded from Pixabay
www.pixabay.com @2019 December 06, 2019
Pixabay GmbH (VAT Reg.No.: DE322857686) p.A. Ruter und Partner Steuerberatungsgesellschaft mbB, Prielmayerstr. 3, 80335 München, Germany

The Decomposition of Waste in Landfills: A Story of Time and Materials
by Rick LeBlanc, Updated October 22, 2019
https://www.thebalancesmb.com/how-long-does-it-take-garbage-to-decompose-2878033

What's SUP: Sasha, Butch, Cuff and Seff, A Single-Used Plastic Story!
Storyline by Glengyl Onga Umali
Solely created for this book project

Team Building Activity Guide Unpublished Manuscript by Glengyl Onga Umali
Originally created in May 2009 for Non-Government Organization's Activity Guide.

You are now a certified EARTH WARRIOR!
Share this story with your friends and
families! Thank you! See you soon!

Glengyl Onga Umali also known as "What's SUP" on YouTube a kid friendly channel. Glengyl took a Bachelor of Arts in Sociology in Mindanao State University – Iligan Institute of Technology (MSU-IIT) – Iligan City, Philippines. He earned a Masteral units in Sustainable Development Studies (MiSDS) major in Sustainable Community Development at the said university and Masteral units in Public Administration in MSU – Marawi.

Mr. Umali is a Sustainable Community Development Advocate, a multi-potentialist having a variety of accomplishments in the field of Community Organizing focusing on Conflict Management and Peace Education in Northwestern Mindanao through Pailig Development Foundation, Incorporated (PDFI). A former workshop facilitator of the Bishop-Ulama Conference – Mindanaw Tripartite Youth Core. (BUC-MTYC). And served as a Secretariat and a Production Staff of The Integrated Performing Arts Guild (IPAG) in Iligan. Having been active in the field of volunteer work in a Non-Government Organization, he was chosen as one of the four

(4) representative from the Philippines during the "Asia – Pacific Forum: Youth Action on Climate Change; Exploration through Cultural Expression" in Rajamangala University of Technology Phra Nakhon in Thailand. He was a SEAMEO-SPAFA scholar from 2010 to 2011.

Printed in the United States
By Bookmasters